Wisdom Unleashed

200 Buddhist Quotes to Guide and Inspire your Life

By

Jamie Jennings

Obadiah N. M.

July 2023

Foreword

In *"Wisdom Unleashed: 200 Buddhist Quotes to Guide and Inspire Your Life,"* we're urged to go on a transforming journey via Buddhist teachings. This unique collection of 200 meaningful quotes illuminates our path and offers significant advice for our personal growth and spiritual development.

This book is a carefully picked collection of famous Buddhist statements that embody the essence of this deep spiritual tradition. Each phrase is a key that opens a universe of thought, revealing insights into the essence of life, the workings of the mind, and the road to awakening.

"Wisdom Unleashed" is a personal invitation to start on a journey of self-discovery and spiritual development. As we read the words and thoughts on these pages, we are reminded that the route to waking is not found in faraway locations or intricate ceremonies, but in our own hearts and brains.

Dear reader, we are honored to provide you with this fascinating compilation: May "Wisdom Unleashed" provide you with inspiration, peace, and direction on your journey of self-discovery and inner change. May these words awaken your hidden knowledge and equip you to negotiate the complexity of life with grace and compassion.

With deepest gratitude and best wishes.

Jamie Jennings
Obadiah N. M.

Contents

CHAPTER 1: Introduction

Welcome to "Wisdom Unleashed: 200 Buddhist Quotes to Guide and Inspire Your Life." Within the pages of this book, you will embark on a transforming journey into the depths of Buddhist knowledge, drawing from a chosen collection of 200 famous Buddhist quotes.

Buddhism, with its rich intellectual teachings and eternal precepts, provides significant insights that can lead us to inner peace, enlightenment, and a more meaningful existence. The words of the Buddha and other enlightened teachers contain great knowledge, providing us with invaluable advice and inspiration as we navigate the difficulties of life.

In this book, we have carefully picked 200 Buddhist quotes that capture the essence of this profound spiritual tradition. Each quotation serves as a portal to deeper thought, asking you to delve into the profound insight contained inside its few words. As you read through these quotations, you will uncover timeless truths that address the common human experience, providing insight on how to overcome pain, cultivate awareness, and achieve harmony in an ever-changing world.

Furthermore, each quote has life lessons that may be applied to your daily life. These courses address a wide range of topics, including mindfulness, compassion, inner growth, self-discovery, and finding serenity in the midst of life's obstacles. You will be encouraged to incorporate the profound teachings of Buddhism into your own life as you explore these statements and their associated insights, creating personal growth, happiness, and a greater sense of purpose.

"Wisdom Unleashed" is intended to be a companion, leading you on your unique journey of self-discovery and development, whether you are new to Buddhism or have been on a spiritual path for some time. Each statement and the thoughts that follow it provide a chance to pause, ponder, and assimilate these timeless principles into our daily life.

We encourage you to join us on this illuminating trip as we look at 200 Buddhist statements that may guide and inspire your life. May this book serve as a lighthouse of insight, guiding you to better understanding, inner serenity, and fulfilment.

Let us begin our journey into the great teachings of Buddhism with open hearts and minds.

CHAPTER 2: About Buddhism: Core values, believes, and practices

Siddhartha Gautama, afterwards known as Buddha, founded Buddhism in India about the 5th century BCE. It is founded on Buddha's teachings and concepts, which aimed to comprehend the nature of suffering and the road to release from it. Buddhism has subsequently expanded to other regions o the world and has millions of adherents.

1.1. Core values and beliefs:

The Four Noble Truths: The Four Noble Truths are the cornerstone o Buddhism, since they accept the presence of suffering (dukkha), identify its causes (craving and attachment), provide a way to end suffering (nirvana) and offer a way to end suffering (the Noble Eightfold Path).

1) **The Noble Eightfold Path:** This path is made up of eigh interwoven principles that assist Buddhists to live ethically and mindfully. Right View, Right Intention, Right Speech, Right Action Right Livelihood, Right Effort, Right Mindfulness, and Righ Concentration are all part of it.

2) **Karma:** Buddhists believe in the law of karma, which states tha actions have repercussions. good activities provide good results whilst bad actions produce negative results, influencing future lives and experiences.

3) **Reincarnation and Nirvana:** Nirvana and reincarnation Buddhism teaches the cycle of birth, death, and rebirth (samsara) The ultimate objective is to achieve Nirvana, a state of perfect enlightenment and emancipation, and therefore be free of this cycle.

4) **Compassion and Non-violence:** Buddhists embrace compassion and nonviolence towards all sentient creatures in order to promote harmony and understanding.

1.2. Practices:

1) **Meditation:** Meditation is central to Buddhist practice and aids in the development of mindfulness, concentration, and insight. Vipassana and Zen meditation are two types of meditation that are practiced.

2) **Offerings and Devotion:** As a demonstration of respect and thanks, Buddhists frequently give offerings to the Buddha and Bodhisattvas. Chanting, prayer, and visits to temples and monasteries are all ways to show one's devotion.

3) **Study of Buddhist Scriptures:** Buddhists study holy books such as the Tripitaka (Pali Canon) and Mahayana sutras to gain a better grasp of Buddha's teachings.

4) **Observing Precepts:** Buddhists adhere to ethical precepts that direct individuals to refrain from destructive activities such as murder, theft, lying, sexual misbehaviour, and drunkenness.

5) **Pilgrimages:** Some Buddhists visit sacred locations related with Buddha's life, such as Bodh Gaya, Lumbini, and Sarnath.

6) **Almsgiving and Charity:** Almsgiving and charitable activities towards the less fortunate demonstrate generosity and compassion.

In a nutshell, Buddhism provides a complex philosophy and method of life centred on comprehending suffering, cultivating compassion, and pursuing enlightenment. Its guiding principles of mindfulness, compassion, and the pursuit of knowledge have inspired many people to live meaningful lives and seek escape from suffering via the Noble Eightfold way and the way to Nirvana.

CHAPTER 3: 200 Buddhist Quotes to Guide and Inspire your Life

Count	200 Buddhist Wisdom Quotes
1	"The mind is everything. What you think, you become."
2	"Three things cannot be long hidden: the sun, the moon, and the truth."
3	"In separateness lies the world's greatest misery; in compassion lies the world's true strength."
4	"Peace comes from within. Do not seek it without."
5	"Chaos is inherent in all compounded things. Strive on with diligence."
6	"Hatred does not cease by hatred, but only by love; this is the eternal rule."
7	"Work out your own salvation. Do not depend

	on others."
8	"Do not overrate what you have received, nor envy others. He who envies others does not obtain peace of mind."
9	"The tongue like a sharp knife... Kills without drawing blood."
10	" Change is never painful. Only resistance to change is painful."
11	"Believe nothing, no matter where you read it or who has said it unless it agrees with your own reason and your own common sense."
12	"Let us rise up and be thankful, for if we didn't learn a lot today, at least we learned a little, and if we didn't learn a little, at least we didn't get sick, and if we got sick, at least we didn't die; so, let us all be thankful."
13	"Your worst enemy cannot harm you as much as your own unguarded thoughts."

14	"Health is the greatest gift, contentment the greatest wealth, faithfulness the best relationship."
15	"The trouble is, you think you have time."
16	"Pain is certain, suffering is optional."
17	"Do not be led by others, awaken your own mind, amass your own experience, and decide for yourself your own path."
18	"Thousands of candles can be lighted from a single candle, and the life of the candle will not be shortened. Happiness never decreases by being shared."
19	"We are shaped by our thoughts; we become what we think. When the mind is pure, joy follows like a shadow that never leaves."
20	"No one saves us but ourselves. No one can and no one may. We ourselves must walk the

	path."
21	"The secret of health for both mind and body is not to mourn for the past, worry about the future, or anticipate troubles, but to live in the present moment wisely and earnestly."
22	"Everything that has a beginning has an ending. Make your peace with that and all will be well."
23	"The only real failure in life is not to be true to the best one knows."
24	"To keep the body in good health is a duty... otherwise we shall not be able to keep our mind strong and clear."
25	"In the end, only three things matter: how much you loved, how gently you lived, and how gracefully you let go of things not meant for you."

26	"Your work is to discover your work and then with all your heart to give yourself to it."
27	"There is no path to happiness: happiness is the path."
28	"To support mother and father, to cherish wife and children, and to be engaged in peaceful occupation — this is the greatest blessing."
29	"You will not be punished for your anger; you will be punished by your anger."
30	"The past is already gone; the future is not yet here. There's only one moment for you to live."
31	"The way to happiness is: keep your heart free from hate, your mind from worry. Live simply, give much. Fill your life with love. Do as you would be done by."
32	"To conquer oneself is a greater victory than to

	conquer thousands in a battle."
33	"Those who have failed to work toward the truth have missed the purpose of living."
34	"Should you find a wise critic to point out your faults, follow him as you would a guide to hidden treasure."
35	"Leave behind confused reactions and become patient as the earth; unmoved by anger, unshaken as a pillar, unperturbed as a clear and quiet pool."
36	"Just as a snake sheds its skin, we must shed our past over and over again."
37	"The world is afflicted by death and decay. But the wise do not grieve, having realized the nature of the world."
38	"The true value of a human being is determined by the measure and the sense in

	which they have obtained liberation from the self."
39	"When the student is ready, the teacher will appear."
40	"Happiness comes when your work and words are of benefit to yourself and others."
41	"Our life is shaped by our mind; we become what we think. Suffering follows an evil thought as the wheels of a cart follow the oxen that draw it. Our life is shaped by our mind; we become what we think. Joy follow a pure thought like a shadow that never leaves."
42	"They blame those who remain silent, they blame those who speak much, they blame those who speak in moderation. There is none in the world who is not blamed."
43	"True love is born from understanding."

44	"If you truly loved yourself, you could never hurt another."
45	"A jug fills drop by drop."
46	"Do not look for a sanctuary in anyone except yourself."
47	"I do not dispute with the world; rather it is the world that disputes with me."
48	"If you are facing in the right direction, all you need to do is keep on walking."
49	"Even death is not to be feared by one who has lived wisely."
50	"Nothing can harm you as much as your own thoughts unguarded."
51	"All that we are is the result of what we have thought. The mind is everything. What we

	think, we become."
52	"Health is the greatest gift, contentment is the greatest wealth."
53	"Be truthful; do not yield to anger. Give freely, even if you have but little. The gods will bless you."
54	"The greatest prayer is patience."
55	"When you like a flower, you just pluck it. But when you love a flower, you water it daily."
56	"A generous heart, kind speech, and a life of service and compassion are the things that renew humanity."
57	"An idea that is developed and put into action is more important than an idea that exists only as an idea."

58	"Don't run after pleasure and neglect the practice of meditation. If you forget the goal of life and get caught in the pleasures of the world, you will come to envy those who put meditation first."
59	"Meditate ... do not delay, lest you later regret it."
60	"You can search throughout the entire universe for someone who is more deserving of your love and affection than you are yourself, and that person is not to be found anywhere. You, yourself, as much as anybody in the entire universe, deserve your love and affection."
61	"To enjoy good health, to bring true happiness to one's family, to bring peace to all, one must first discipline and control one's own mind. If a man can control his mind, he can find the

way to Enlightenment, and all wisdom and virtue will naturally come to him."

62	"Words have the power to both destroy and heal. When words are both true and kind, they can change our world."
63	" Meditate. Live purely. Be quiet. Do your work with mastery. Like the moon, come out from behind the clouds! Shine."
64	" Before you speak, let your words pass through three gates: Is it true? Is it necessary? Is it kind?"
65	"As I am, so are these. As are these, so am I. Drawing the parallel to yourself, neither kill nor get others to kill."
66	"Do not pray for an easy life, pray for the strength to endure a difficult one."

67	"If a man going down into a river, swollen and swiftly flowing, is carried away by the current — how can he help others across?"
68	"Those who are free of resentful thoughts surely find peace."
69	"When you attain victory over yourself, not even the gods can turn it into defeat."
70	"Happiness will never come to those who fail to appreciate what they already have."
71	"Holding onto anger is like drinking poison and expecting the other person to die."
72	"The quieter you become, the more you can hear."
73	"The foot feels the foot when it feels the ground."
74	"If your compassion does not include yourself,

	it is incomplete."
75	"If you are quiet enough, you will hear the flow of the universe. You will feel its rhythm. Go with this flow. Happiness lies ahead. Meditation is key."
76	"The less you want, the richer you are. The more you give, the wealthier you become."
77	"Happiness does not depend on what you have or who you are. It solely relies on what you think."
78	"Just as a solid rock is not shaken by the storm, even so the wise are not affected by praise or blame."
79	"Those who cling to perceptions and views wander the world offending people."
80	"The present moment is the only moment available to us, and it is the door to all

	moments."
81	"It is better to do nothing, than to do what is wrong. For whatever you do, you do to yourself."
82	"You only lose what you cling to."
83	"You must love yourself before you love another. By accepting yourself and fully being what you are, your simple presence can make others happy."
84	"If you knew what I know about the power of giving, you would not let a single meal pass without sharing it in some way."
85	"Everything that happens to us is the result of what we ourselves have thought, said, or done. We alone are responsible for our lives."
86	"Remembering a wrong is like carrying a burden on the mind."

87	"Conquer anger with non-anger. Conquer badness with goodness. Conquer meanness with generosity. Conquer dishonesty with truth."
88	" Happiness does not depend on what you have or who you are. It solely relies on what you think."
89	"What is evil? Killing is evil, lying is evil, slandering is evil, abuse is evil, gossip is evil, envy is evil, hatred is evil, to cling to false doctrine is evil; all these things are evil. And what is the root of evil? Desire is the root of evil, illusion is the root of evil."
90	"What you think you become. What you feel you attract. What you imagine you create."
91	"You are far from the end of your journey. The way is not in the sky. The way is in the heart. See how you love."

92	" There are only two mistakes one can make along the road to truth; not going all the way, and not starting."
93	"All conditioned things are impermanent—when one sees this with wisdom, one turns away from suffering."
94	"It is a man's own mind, not his enemy or foe, that lures him to evil ways."
95	"Everything is changeable, everything appears and disappears; there is no blissful peace until one passes beyond the agony of life and death."
96	"You cannot travel the path until you have become the path itself."
97	"One who conquers himself is greater than another who conquers a thousand times a thousand men on the battlefield. Be victorious

	over yourself and not over others."
98	"Suffering is not holding you, you are holding suffering."
99	"All things appear and disappear because of the concurrence of causes and conditions. Nothing ever exists entirely alone; everything is in relation to everything else."
100	"Ceasing to do evil, Cultivating the good, Purifying the heart: This is the teaching of the Buddhas."
101	"To understand everything is to forgive everything."
102	"Health is the best gift, contentment the best wealth, trust the best kinsman, nirvana the greatest joy. Drink the nectar of the dharma in the depths of meditation, and become free from fear and sin."

103	"Your work is to discover your world and then with all your heart give yourself to it."
104	"There is nothing more dreadful than the habit of doubt. Doubt separates people. It is a poison that disintegrates friendships and breaks up pleasant relations. It is a thorn that irritates and hurts; it is a sword that kills."
105	"When one has the feeling of dislike for evil, when one feels tranquil, one finds pleasure in listening to good teachings; when one has these feelings and appreciates them, one is free of fear."
106	"Happiness is not having a lot. Happiness is giving a lot."
107	"Do not dwell in the past; do not dream of the future; concentrate the mind on the present moment."

108	"Holding on to anger is like grasping a hot coal with the intent of throwing it at someone else; you are the one who gets burned."
109	"All wrong-doing arises because of mind. If mind is transformed can wrong-doing remain?"
110	"If you meditate earnestly, pure in mind and kind in deeds, leading a disciplined life in harmony with the dharma, you will grow in glory. If you meditate earnestly, through spiritual disciplines you can make an island for yourself that no flood can overwhelm."
111	"Anger will never disappear so long as thoughts of resentment are cherished in the mind. Anger will disappear as soon as thoughts of resentment are forgotten."
112	"If you want to fly, give up everything that weighs you down."

113	"Be where you are; otherwise, you will miss your life."
114	"Nothing is forever except change."
115	"If we could see the miracle of a single flower clearly, our whole life would change."
116	"Just as treasures are uncovered from the earth, so virtue appears from good deeds, and wisdom appears from a pure and peaceful mind. To walk safely through the maze of human life, one needs the light of wisdom and the guidance of virtue."
117	"The whole secret of existence is to have no fear. Never fear what will become of you, depend on no one. Only the moment you reject all help are you freed."
118	" What you think, you become. What you feel, you attract. What you imagine, you create."

119	" Pain is inevitable. Suffering is optional."
120	"It seems that although we thought ourselves permanent, we are not. Although we thought ourselves settled, we are not. Although we thought we would last forever, we will not."
121	"The root of suffering is attachment."
122	"Let him not deceive another nor despise anyone anywhere. In anger or ill will let him not wish another ill."
123	"One is not called noble who harms living beings. By not harming living beings one is called noble."
124	"Better than a thousand hollow words, is one word that brings peace."
125	"When you realize how perfect everything is, you will tilt your head back and laugh at the sky."

126	"Teach this triple truth to all: A generous heart, kind speech, and a life of service and compassion are the things which renew humanity."
127	"The one in whom no longer exist the craving and thirst that perpetuate becoming; how could you track that Awakened one, trackless, and of limitless range?"
128	"All suffering is caused by ignorance. People inflict pain on others in the selfish pursuit of their own happiness or satisfaction."
129	"Train your eyes and ears; train your nose and tongue. The senses are good friends when they are trained. Train your body in deeds, train your tongue in words, train your mind in thoughts. This training will take you beyond sorrow."
130	"To keep the body in good health is a duty;

otherwise, we shall not be able to keep the mind strong and clear."

131 " Every morning we are born again. What we do today is what matters most."

132 "You yourself, as much as anybody in the entire universe, deserve your love and affection."

133 "If anything is worth doing, do it with all your heart."

134 "Neither fire, nor wind, birth, nor death, can erase our good deeds."

135 "There is no fear for one whose mind is not filled with desires."

136 "Your own self is your master; who else could be? With yourself well controlled, you gain a master very hard to find."

137 "Whatever has the nature of arising has the

nature of ceasing."

138	"Better it is to live one day seeing the rise and fall of things than to live a hundred years without ever seeing the rise and fall of things."
139	"All tremble at violence; all fear death. Putting oneself in the place of another, one should not kill nor cause another to kill."
140	"It is easy to see the faults of others, but difficult to see one's own faults. One shows the faults of others like chaff winnowed in the wind, but one conceals one's own faults as a cunning gambler conceals his dice."
141	"What we think, we become."
142	"Virtue is persecuted more by the wicked than it is loved by the good."
143	"I will not look at another's bowl intent on

	finding fault: a training to be observed."
144	"The wise one's fashioned speech with their thought, sifting it as grain is sifted through a sieve."
145	"Meditation brings wisdom; lack of meditation leaves ignorance."
146	"If with a pure mind a person speaks or acts, happiness follows them like a never-departing shadow."
147	"If the problem can be solved why worry? If the problem cannot be solved worrying will do you no good."
148	"Purity or impurity depends on oneself. No one can purify another."
149	"Life is suffering."
150	"Should a person do good, let him do it again and again. Let him find pleasure therein, for

	blissful is the accumulation of good."
151	"Endurance is one of the most difficult disciplines, but it is to the one who endures that the final victory comes."
152	"Conquer anger through gentleness, unkindness through kindness, greed through generosity, and falsehood by truth."
153	" In the end, only three things matter: how much you loved, how gently you lived, and how gracefully you let go of things not meant for you."
154	"In the sky, there is no distinction of east and west; people create distinctions out of their own minds and then believe them to be true."
155	"We are what we think. All that we are arises with our thoughts. With our thoughts, we

	make the world."
156	" Purity or impurity depends on oneself, no one can purify another."
157	"Understanding is the heartwood of well-spoken words."
158	"Just as the great ocean has one taste, the taste of salt, so also this teaching and discipline has one taste, the taste of liberation."
159	"In whom there is no sympathy for living beings: know him as an outcast."
160	" If you want to fly, give up everything that weighs you down."
161	"The only way to do great work is to love what you do."
162	"Purity and impurity depend on oneself; no one can purify another."

163	"Faith and prayer both are invisible, but they make impossible things possible."
164	"We will develop love, we will practice it, we will make it both a way and a basis..."
165	"Like someone pointing to treasure is the wise person who sees your faults and points them out. Associate with such a sage."
166	"There has to be evil so that good can prove its purity above it."
167	"Meditation brings wisdom; lack of meditation leaves ignorance. Know well what leads you forward and what hold you back, and choose the path that leads to wisdom."
168	"Whatever is not yours: let go of it. Your letting go of it will be for your long-term happiness & benefit."

169	"Your task is not to seek for love, but merely to seek and find all the barriers within yourself that you have built against it."
170	"A man is not called wise because he talks and talks again; but if he is peaceful, loving, and fearless then he is in truth called wise."
171	"One moment can change a day, one day can change a life, and one life can change the world."
172	"Set your heart on doing good. Do it over and over again, and you will be filled with joy."
173	" Quiet! the mind and the soul will speak."
174	"As rain falls equally on the just and the unjust, do not burden your heart with judgement but rain your kindness equally on all."

175	"To conquer oneself is a greater victory than to conquer thousands in a battle."
176	"Know from the rivers in clefts and in crevices: those in small channels flow noisily, the great flow silent. Whatever's not full makes noise. Whatever is full is quiet."
177	"Love the whole world as a mother loves her only child."
178	" If we fail to look after others when they need help, who will look after us?"
179	" Whatever words we utter should be chosen with care for people will hear them and be influenced by them for good or ill."
180	"To live a pure unselfish life, one must count nothing as one's own in the midst of abundance."
181	"A disciplined mind brings happiness."

182	"Your worst enemy cannot harm you as much as your own thoughts, unguarded. But once mastered, No one can help you as much, not even your father or your mother."
183	"Drop by drop is the water pot filled. Likewise, the wise man, gathering it little by little, fills himself with good."
184	" Believe nothing, no matter where you read it, or who said it, no matter if I have said it, unless it agrees with your own reason and your own common sense."
185	"Ardently do today what must be done. Who knows? Tomorrow, death comes."
186	Like a fine flower, beautiful to look at but without scent, fine words are fruitless in a man who does not act in accordance with them."
187	"As an elephant in the battlefield withstands

	arrows shot from bows all around, even so shall I endure abuse."
188	" Avoid evil deeds as a man who loves life avoids poison."
189	"Let none find fault with others; let none see the omissions and commissions of others. But let one see one's own acts, done and undone."
190	"You only lose what you cling to."
191	"It is in the nature of things that joy arises in a person free from remorse."
192	"However, many holy words you read, however many you speak, what good will they do you If you do not act upon them?"
193	" When it hurts, observe. Life is trying to teach you something."
194	"Nothing remains without change."

195	"Not by rituals and resolutions, nor by much learning, nor by celibacy, nor even by meditation can you find the supreme, immortal joy of nirvana until you extinguish your self-will."
196	" Happiness will never come to those who fail to appreciate what they already have."
197	"If you light a lamp for someone else it will also brighten your path."
198	"If you do not change direction, you may end up where you are heading."
199	"Whatever is not yours: let go of it. Your letting go of it will be for your long-term happiness & benefit."
200	"Good people keep on walking whatever happens. They do not speak vain words and

are the same in good fortune and bad. If one desires neither children nor wealth nor power nor success by unfair means, know such a one to be good, wise, and virtuous."

CHAPTER 4: 50 Key Buddhist Concepts and their Relevance in Daily Life

1) **Metta (Loving-Kindness):** Cultivating unconditional love and goodwill towards all beings, promoting harmony and compassion.

2) **Karuna (Compassion):** Showing empathy and concern for the suffering of others, and actively seeking to alleviate their pain.

3) **Mudita (Sympathetic Joy):** Finding joy in the happiness and success of others, without envy or jealousy.

4) **Upekkha (Equanimity):** Maintaining mental balance and composure, especially in challenging situations.

5) **Samsara:** The cycle of birth, death, and rebirth, symbolizing th continuous journey of existence.

6) **Nirvana:** The ultimate goal in Buddhism, representing liberatio from suffering and the cessation of rebirth.

7) **Anicca (Impermanence):** The understanding that all things ar impermanent and subject to change.

8) **Anatta (Non-Self):** The concept that there is no permanen unchanging self or soul; everything is interconnected and constantl changing.

9) **Dukkha (Suffering):** The recognition of the inheren dissatisfaction and unsatisfactoriness in life, motivating the searcl for liberation.

10) **Sangha:** The Buddhist community of monks, nuns, anc practitioners who support and guide each other in their spiritua journey.

11) **Dharma:** The teachings of Buddha, representing the ultimate trutl and the path to enlightenment.

12) **Bodhisattva:** An enlightened being who chooses to remain in the cycle of rebirth to help others attain enlightenment.

13) **Sila (Ethical Conduct):** Observance of moral precepts anc principles that guide one's actions towards non-harming and ethical behavior.

14) **Mara:** Symbolizes the embodiment of desire, delusion, and death representing inner obstacles on the path to enlightenment.

15) **Pratityasamutpada (Dependent Origination):** The concept that all things arise in dependence on various causes and conditions.

16) **Upadana (Clinging):** The attachment and grasping to desires and

worldly phenomena that perpetuate suffering.

17) **Samadhi (Concentration):** The state of focused and one-pointed mind achieved through meditation practices.

18) **Anapanasati (Mindfulness of Breathing):** A meditation technique focusing on the breath to cultivate mindfulness and concentration.

19) **Prajna (Wisdom):** The development of insight and understanding, leading to the realization of the nature of reality.

20) **Karma:** The law of cause and effect, where actions have consequences and influence future experiences and rebirth.

21) **Dana (Generosity):** The practice of giving and sharing selflessly, cultivating a generous heart.

22) **Upasana (Devotion):** Deep reverence and dedication to the Buddha, Dharma, and Sangha.

23) **Maraṇasati (Mindfulness of Death):** Contemplation of mortality to appreciate the impermanence of life and live with purpose.

24) **Piti (Rapture):** A blissful and uplifting feeling experienced during deep meditation.

25) **Sutta:** Buddhist scriptures containing the teachings of the Buddha.

26) **Vinaya:** The monastic code of discipline governing the conduct of monks and nuns.

27) **Bhavana (Mental Cultivation):** The practice of meditation and mental development.

28) **Sati (Mindfulness):** Cultivating awareness and presence in daily activities.

29) **Noble Truths:** The fundamental truths about the nature of suffering and the path to its cessation.

30) **Samskara (Mental Formation):** Mental habits and conditioning that shape behavior and experiences.

31) **Skandhas (Aggregates):** The five components that constitute the individual: form, sensation, perception, mental formations, and consciousness.

32) **Bhikkhu/Bhikkhuni:** A fully ordained Buddhist monk/nun following the monastic path.

33) **Stupa:** A sacred monument or shrine containing relics or significant artifacts.

34) **Sila-Samadhi-Prajna:** The threefold training of ethics, concentration, and wisdom.

35) **Tanha (Craving):** The attachment and desire that lead to suffering.

36) **Bhava (Becoming):** The process of being reborn into different states of existence.

37) **Jhana (Meditative Absorption):** Deep states of meditative concentration.

38) **Bhumi (Stages of Enlightenment):** The ten stages a Bodhisattva passes through on the path to Buddhahood.

39) **Anupadisesa-Nibbana:** The complete cessation of suffering and rebirth, attained upon death.

40) **Paccekabuddha:** A "silent" or "solitary" Buddha who attains enlightenment without teaching others.

41) **Tathagata:** An epithet for Buddha, meaning "one who has thus gone" or "one who has thus come."

42) **Paramita (Perfection):** Virtues or practices that lead to enlightenment, like generosity, patience, and wisdom.

43) **Satipatthana (Four Foundations of Mindfulness):** Meditative practices focusing on mindfulness of body, feelings, mind, and mental objects.

44) **Sutta Pitaka:** The "Basket of Discourses," a collection of Buddha's teachings.

45) **Abhidhamma:** The higher teachings or philosophical analysis of Buddhist doctrine.

46) **Anupubbikatha (Gradual Instruction):** The gradual and systematic teaching of Dharma to spiritual aspirants.

47) **Bhava-Chakra (Wheel of Life):** A symbolic representation of the cycle of existence and the twelve links of dependent origination.

48) **Brahma-Viharas (Four Immeasurables):** Practices of loving-kindness, compassion, sympathetic joy, and equanimity.

49) **Vesak (Buddha Day):** A major Buddhist festival celebrating the birth, enlightenment, and death of Buddha.

50) **Kasina (Meditation Objects):** Physical objects used in meditation to cultivate concentration and mental focus.

CHAPTER 5: Your personal Reflection Section

Welcome to the Personal Reflection Section of this wisdom book. Here you will discover blank pages and parts dedicated to encouraging your personal interaction with the quotes and offering room for your own creativity, and documentation.

The goal of this section is to urge you to actively engage in the quotes experience, to delve deeper into your own spiritual path, and to build a personal relationship with the divine. It is a chance for you to communicate your ideas, emotions, and wishes in a reflective and private manner.

So, in this space, feel free to practice your meditation, entrust yourself on the truths and teachings provided in these quotes, and to explore your own wisdom. You can meditate deeply and write down your own quote as you embark on the journey of wisdom.

1 Setting your Goals	2 What needs to be done to achieve it?	3 Implementation and follow-ups	4 Remarks and updates

About the Authors

Jamie Jennings and Obadiah N. M are well-known writers, specialists, and researchers who have made major contributions to the disciplines of social wisdom, interpersonal relationships with the focus on love and human social interaction, and effective social communication. Their combined efforts have had a significant influence on how individuals perceive and negotiate interpersonal relationships and communication.

Jamie Jennings is an experienced psychologist and communication professional who is fascinated by the complexities of human behavior. Jennings, who has a degree in counselling and psychology, has spent decades researching how people interact, communicate, and build lasting connections. Their profound insights into the human mind have proven beneficial in assisting individuals in forging stronger friendships and developing harmonious relationships.

Obadiah N. M is a renowned economics and social analysts, noted for his in-depth research on social dynamics, wisdom acquisition, and the nature of love in human relationships. N. M's work sheds light on the role of empathy, compassion, and emotional intelligence in promoting healthy communities and personal connections by drawing on ancient philosophies and mixing them with current sociological theories.

Jamie Jennings and Obadiah N. M have collaborated on numerous pioneering publications that have received international acclaim. Their writings smoothly mix scientific research, philosophical insight, and practical counsel, allowing their expertise to be accessible to a broad audience.

Obadiah N. M. and Jamie Jennings continue to push the frontiers of social intelligence and effective communication. Their commitment to understanding the human experience and enhancing relationships has given them a place of honor in the profession, motivating many people to live more fulfilled live.

www.ingramcontent.com/pod-product-compliance
Lightning Source LLC
Chambersburg PA
CBHW062248290526
45794CB00006B/2464